ULTRAMARATHONS

★★★ *The World's* ★★★
Most Punishing Races

ULTRAMARATHONS

★★★ The World's ★★★ Most Punishing Races

Nate Aaseng

Lerner Publications Company
Minneapolis

Front cover: The lead runners in the tough Western States 100 will pass Cougar Rock (lower right) several hours following their 5:00 A.M. start.
Back cover: More than 10,000 runners mass at the start of South Africa's Comrades Marathon, eager to take up the challenge of the world's largest ultramarathon.
Page 1: The "thrill of victory" is nowhere to be seen on the face of Sylviane Puntous (center), an Ironman Triathlon champion. Her celebration will have to wait until she feels human again.
Page 2: Gritty determination carries runners along for much of the climb in the Pike's Peak Marathon. The photograph on page six shows what happens after the grueling terrain has taken its toll.

To Jay Johnson
for his help in making a research project possible.

Library of Congress Cataloging-in-Publication Data

Aaseng, Nathan.
    Ultramarathons : the world's most punishing races.

    (Sports talk)
    Summary: Describes the history of ultramarathons and
highlights eight of the most exhausting modern-day races
including The Torturous 26, The Ironman Triathlon, and
The Nanisivik Midnight Sun Ultra.
    1. Marathon running—Juvenile literature. [1. Marathon
running. 2. Running] I. Title. II. Series.
GV1065.A18   1987   796.4'26   87-2896
ISBN 0-8225-1534-2 (lib. bdg.)

Manufactured in the United States of America

  2   3   4   5   6   7   8   9   10   97   96   95   94   93   92   91   90   89   88

★★★ Contents ★★★

	Introduction	7
1	**The Ironman Triathlon**	11
2	**The Western States 100**	19
3	**The Pike's Peak Marathon**	31
4	**The Comrades Marathon**	39
5	**The Nanisivik Midnight Sun Ultra**	45
6	**The Torturous 26**	51
7	**The Grand Canyon Double Traverse**	57
8	**The Rarahipa**	65

After spending all of his strength on the Pike's Peak course, this runner has to be helped away from the finish line.

Introduction

For many years, the marathon was considered the ultimate athletic torture. Most people could not imagine why runners would want to drag their bodies through a course that is 26 miles and 385 yards long. The few racers who tried the event were either congratulated for their guts or pitied for their stupidity.

This once-shunned event, however, has now become too easy for many runners and instead is used as a *warm-up* for a really tough race—or even as a way to *relax*. These people take on challenges so far beyond the usual marathon that even their closest friends think they are absolutely crazy.

What makes runners want to push their bodies to a point of pain and exhaustion that most people cannot imagine? Simply, it is the challenge of seeing if they can do it. Humans have always tested their limits by seeing how fast and how far they could go. When the marathon became so popular that more than 20,000 runners would enter a single race, it became obvious the

event was not the extreme torture many had believed it to be. There had to be a new challenge—a tougher test of human limits in distance running. And, sure enough, race organizers have had no trouble inventing endurance tests so cruel that one cringes to just read about them.

This book is about some of the most inhumane footraces ever dreamed up. Incredible as it may seem, every brutal race in this book is a well-established running event, with no shortage of people willing to spend their time and/or money for the chance to compete!

Actually, the notion of "ultramarathons" has been around for many years. For centuries, the Tarahumara Indians have scheduled such races as a routine part of their lives. In the Western world, six-day races were a common sport from 1875 to 1888. These were indoor affairs, involving professional runners who earned up to $30,000 for a winning effort. During one classic duel, Charles Rowell and Patrick Fitzgerald slogged

As shown by the strange assortment of shoes and clothing, many contestants in the 1928 Bunion Derby didn't really know what they were getting into.

along the track for over 600 miles before Rowell finally claimed a painful victory.

One March day in 1928, 199 starters showed up at a Los Angeles starting line for the fabulous Bunion Derby. Great riches were promised to the first person who finished the 3,422-mile race across the United States to New York City. Although the race organizers never came up with the money they had promised, 55 weary contestants earned the satisfaction of finishing the course.

Such events, however, were viewed primarily as freak shows. Except for a handful of hardy souls, U.S. runners stayed with shorter events and ignored the growing popularity of ultramarathons in other countries. Such well-established events as the 52-mile London-to-Brighton Run; the 100-kilometer race in Biel, Switzerland; and the 90-kilometer Comrades Marathon in South Africa were virtually unknown in the United States. Although these races attracted hundreds, even thousands, of contestants each year, in 1969, it was estimated that fewer than 70 U.S. runners took on the challenge of a long race.

The marathon boom of the 1970s, however, pushed hundreds of thrill-seeking runners into the more incredible races. By 1979, the number of ultra-contestants had grown to nearly 2,500. With television covering new running events such as the Hawaii Ironman and the Western States 100, the number of competitors exploded beyond belief. It is estimated that nearly 1.1 million contestants participated in the grueling triathlon competitions held in the United States in 1985. Many of the top endurance runs, such as the Pike's Peak Marathon, had to turn away runners to keep from overcrowding the course.

This book highlights some of the most exhausting races held in the world today. Included are only those races that are repeated regularly at a single location. Therefore, some of the most lethal runs attempted, such as one through the stifling heat of Death Valley, are not mentioned. That 146-mile course from Badwater, California—the lowest point in the United States—to Mt. Whitney—

the highest—has the potential to outdo all of the other races in this book. But so far, few runners have felt challenged to run through 135-degree (Fahrenheit) heat, so the run has rarely been attempted.

There have also been other courageous runs across Canada and the United States: 24-hour races, six-day races, and 24-hour endless relays. But because many of them are run on a track instead of a standardized course and are not regulary scheduled events, they have not been included either.

No doubt, we have not seen the end of the search for the world's toughest footrace. Perhaps someone will come up with a race across the Saraha Desert, around the Dead Sea, across the Polar ice cap, or up and down Mt. Everest. But no matter how tough a race one can dream up, it seems there will always be a pack of runners at the starting line, ready to give it a go.

Here, then, are eight of the most famous and most demanding footraces. Judge for yourself. Are the runners who tackle these events extremely brave or just plain crazy?

She made it, but not by much! This Ironman finisher found the race every bit as tough as it had been promised.

★★★1★★★
The Ironman Triathlon

Late in 1977, Navy commander John Collins and some of his friends were cooling off after taking part in one of Hawaii's many "fun runs." They started talking about the variety of tough challenges on the island, such as the Waikiki Rough Water swim, the bike race around Oahu, and the Honolulu Marathon.

Before long, the friends were arguing about which group was more fit—swimmers, bikers, or runners. Collins thought the best way to decide would be to combine all three events into a single race. That idea was worth a good laugh at the time. After all, who in their right mind would even attempt such a feat? As it turned out, a handful of dedicated athletes had competed in scattered "triathlon" events since the 1960s.

When the idea of the Ironman Triathlon was announced the next year, however, Collins discovered 14 men and

1 woman who were ready to take on the challenge. In spite of enormous ocean waves whipped up by gales more than 40 miles an hour, the challengers could hardly wait to get started. The race was postponed for one day until the weather calmed down, and then the first Ironman Triathlon was under way.

The idea of swimming 2.4 miles, biking 112 miles, and then running 26.2 miles—all without a break—seemed so unbelievable that *Sports Illustrated* magazine sent a reporter to cover the event. He looked on in awe as 12 of the 15 starters staggered to the finish line. (The winner was a 28-year-old ex-cabdriver.) Two years later, a television crew from ABC's *Wide World of Sports* filmed this Hawaiian madness. Unbelievably, the field had then grown to 108 iron-willed athletes.

That 1980 race included a finish so gripping that those who were watching broke into tears. Julie Moss shuffled toward the finish line a few minutes ahead of the next female competitor. One-quarter mile from the end of the race, she fell to the ground. Almost numb from the day-long effort, she took three minutes to get back on her feet. Moss then made it to within 100 yards of the finish and collapsed again. Staggering forward, she collapsed still another time and then once more only 15 feet away from victory. Totally exhausted, she saw her rival, Kathleen McCartney, jog past her to gain the victory. Still, Moss crawled along until she finally dragged herself the last 15 feet to the finish to take second place. Veteran sportscasters called it the most courageous effort they had ever seen in sports.

Boosted by television coverage and inspired by Julie Moss, Hawaii's Triathlon —still commonly called the Ironman despite the many women entrants—grew too big for the island of Oahu. In 1981, the 400 racers were moved to the larger island of Hawaii. A year later, there were more than 800 starters and, by 1983, hundreds had to be turned away to keep the field at a manageable 1,200! The triathlon had become so competitive that only two finishers in the first race would have qualified in 1983.

Those who are awarded a spot in the race join the crowd of hearty competitors on the white sand beaches of Kailua Bay. When the gun goes off, there is a mad dash into the water and a flurry of splashing. With so many people in the water, swimmers are constantly bumping into each other, and it takes quite some time before they can gain any speed. As they swim toward the glass-bottomed boat that is the halfway marker, they have to check every few strokes to see if the winds and the strong waves have pushed them off course. As any ocean swimmer knows, there is always the danger of wandering into the painful sting of a jellyfish. And salt water can get in the eyes, making it difficult to see. Worse yet, swallowing water could give a competitor a queasy stomach, which could make the later long bike ride and run absolutely unbearable. There have been pleasant surprises in the water, though, such as the time the leaders found themselves swimming among a group of playful dolphins!

Ironman rules have been tightened so that anyone still in the water after

Like a pack of frenzied sharks, nearly 1,000 athletes churn through the water on the first leg of what is now called the Bud Light Ironman.

two hours is disqualified. Once out of the water, the racers head for showers in brightly colored tents. Hundreds of volunteers are on hand to help them change, find their bikes, and start peddling on the second leg of their journey.

No sooner do the racers jump on their bikes than they are faced with a steep, quarter-mile hill. For the next 112 miles, they journey through fascinating scenery, including a black lava desert and towering, 13,000-foot volcanoes. They do not, however, see a variety of plant life, for few plants are able to grow in the miles and miles of crusty lava. As the bikers follow the two-lane highway, baked by the sun on shadeless ground, they often feel they are riding through an endless oven. Along with the heat and the increasing ache of

Although they may be bucking headwinds of up to 55 miles per hour, Ironman triathletes may be disqualified if they let another biker break the wind for them.

fatigued muscles, they also have to battle monotony. For a long stretch, every mile looks the same, giving bikers the feeling they will never reach the end. There is also little to stop the strong head winds that make pedaling so difficult. Gusts of Pacific winds have been known to blow the front wheels of even the heaviest bikers clear off the ground!

All of the training of some triathletes goes to waste, though, when their bike breaks down in the middle of a race. Others discover that the two miles of kicking during their ocean swim causes muscle cramps when they pedal. For these reasons, there are aid stations every five miles along the course. A weary racer can find food, drink, music, and even a massage at any of them.

Once the biking course has been completed, it's on to the marathon. The faster bikers and swimmers begin running in the hottest part of the day, so wise contestants drink and eat as much as they can while biking and running to keep from being dehydrated. But nothing can fight off complete exhaustion from such effort in the heat. Runners have been known to stumble into parked cars, to get confused or lost, or to babble complete nonsense as they plod along. With some luck and an enormous amount of effort, though, they move into the final leg of the race, which carries them along the sea wall to the finish line back at the pier. Winners can complete the course in just under 9 hours. The remaining contestants have 17 hours in which to finish before the race is declared over.

After that ordeal, few racers feel like talking, and it usually takes many hours before they even feel human again. So why do they do it? The only prize for the winner is a five-inch trophy made from nuts and bolts, the symbol of the world's top Iron Man or Iron Woman.

Scott Tinley finished the 1985 Ironman in a world record time of 8 hours, 50 minutes, 54 seconds.

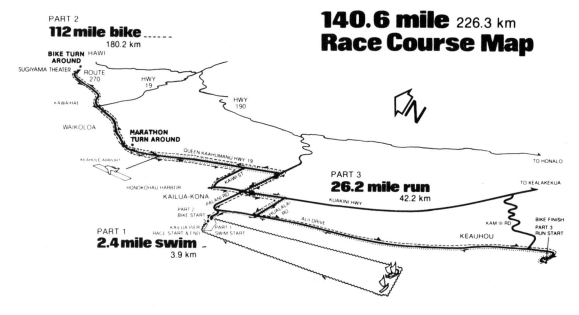

PART 2
112 mile bike ......
180.2 km

BIKE TURN
AROUND · HAWI
SUGIYAMA THEATER · ROUTE
270

HWY
19

140.6 mile 226.3 km
Race Course Map

HWY
190

KAWAIHAE

WAIKOLOA

**MARATHON
TURN AROUND**

QUEEN KAAHUMANU HWY 19

KEAHOLE AIRPORT

HONOKOHAU HARBOR

KAILUA-KONA

PART 2
BIKE START

KAILUA PIER
RACE START & END

PART 1
SWIM START

PART 1
2.4 mile swim .
3.9 km

KAIWI ST.

PALANI RD.

HUALALAI RD.

ALII DRIVE

PART 3
26.2 mile run
42.2 km

KUAKINI HWY

TO HONALO

TO KEALAKEKUA

KAM III RD.

KEAUHOU

BIKE FINISH
PART 3
RUN START

All three phases of the Ironman are down and back courses along the coast of the island of Hawaii.

That's hardly worth the $100 entry fee and the expense of traveling to Hawaii with a support crew to help get them through the race. Nor can it be worth the pain and effort of training six to eight hours a day and running 70 miles, biking 400 miles, and swimming 18 miles a week. Still, there is something about racing in a triathlon that makes total strangers feel close to each other as they battle tremendous odds. Perhaps more importantly, the thrill of finishing a triathlon gives participants a sense of satisfaction that can last for the rest of their lives.

In 1986, Dave Scott, here shown savoring his 1984 win, shattered Tinley's record with a time of 8 hours, 28 minutes, 37 seconds.

Victims of the Western States 100 course can blame this man, Wendell Robie, for dreaming up the race. In his defense, Robie intended the race to be for horses, not humans.

★★★2★★★
The Western States 100

Those who have sampled the worst the running world has to offer declare that the Western States 100 tops all other races for sheer agony. They say there is no way to imagine what that race can do to you. After surveying all of the world's most grueling races, *Outside* magazine judged it the toughest endurance contest ever devised.

The race started innocently enough back in 1955 when a California banker named Wendell T. Robie wanted to prove modern horses were just as rugged as the sturdy steeds that had carried the mail for the old Pony Express. Robie rode his horse over a brutal stretch of the Sierra Nevada Mountains in California. This rocky Indian trail had been used by miners traveling from the silver mines of Nevada to California's gold mines.

Robie's 100-mile ride from Squaw Valley to Auburn was organized as an annual horse race and called the Tevis Cup. It might have remained a horse race had not Gordy Ainsleigh's horse come up lame on race day in 1974. Determined not to be left out of the "fun," Ainsleigh decided he would attempt the race on foot the following year.

Gordy must have cursed his decision a thousand times as he ran over the harsh terrain, especially when he came upon a horse that had collapsed and died from heat and exhaustion. But to the astonishment of the race spectators, Gordy not only finished the course, he did it in just under 24 hours, the original goal set by Robie for a horse and a rider!

In 1975 and 1976, there were lone runners who imitated Ainsleigh's run. After that, the race was made an annual event for human racers, which must have been welcome news to the horses!

19

After 21 miles of mountain running, racers reach Cougar Rock (right foreground). For these rugged souls, the "fun" has barely begun.

Within a decade, U.S. runners' thirst for the ultimate challenge had changed the Western States 100 from a friendly race among local adventure seekers to an event that was almost too big to handle. National coverage, including a television documentary, attracted so many people that race directors were forced to turn away hundreds of applicants. Even with the field limited to 372 runners in 1984, the expense of operating the race was enormous. Over $50,000 and more than 800 volunteers were needed to make sure the race was run safely and smoothly.

Only those in the absolute best of health are allowed on the course. The race, in fact, is so dangerous that all contestants must wear a hospital wrist band giving all important medical information about themselves. There are five checkpoints along the way, and, at each one, runners are examined and their blood, urine, pulse, and blood pressure are tested. Anyone who fails at any point is immediately pulled from the race. In 1985, doctors at the 73-mile check point had to pull 26 dazed runners off the course.

But even with all of these precautions, the Western States 100 is filled

Not trusting the judgement of anyone who would even think of entering such a race, medical officials have the final say as to whether or not a runner is fit enough to continue.

One hundred miles would be punishing enough on dry land, but Western States 100 racers must also plow through slippery snow.

with risks. Running a 100-mile race would be a strain under ideal conditions, but the terrain of this race is miserable. It starts in Squaw Valley, home of the 1980 Winter Olympics, which is surrounded by patches of snow throughout the year. Some years, runners have had to charge through fields of snow for 20 to 30 miles, facing drifts as deep as six feet. The snow makes it so slippery that broken bones from long falls are not uncommon.

Although the course begins at an elevation of 6,000 feet and ends at 1,000 feet, it is far from a "downhill" trail. The terrain is so steep that runners climb a total of 17,000 feet—more than 3 miles—and descend a total of 22,000 feet. Temperatures range from 25 degrees (Fahrenheit) in the upper peaks to about 110 degrees in the lower canyons. There is also the danger of running through bear and rattlesnake country. Because the course is almost impassable with a vehicle, the only way to bring an injured runner to safety is by helicopter.

Before dawn on race day, runners arrive at Squaw Valley accompanied by the music of bagpipes. At 5:00 A.M., they stand poised at the starting line,

Western 100 runners start out before sunrise. Many will still be racing long after sundown.

preparing for the most harrowing experience of their lives. Most are quiet and nervous as they think about what they are about to go through. As the runners are sent on their way, they have to be careful not to let their excitement get the best of them. Many a top runner has paid for the mistake of starting out too fast by collapsing near the 70-mile mark.

The race begins with a 3,000-foot climb to Emmigrant Gap, the highest point on the course. All but the most confident racers walk this uphill stretch. At this point, they are fresh enough to enjoy the sight of the sun rising over beautiful Red Star Ridge. But they have to pay attention to the winding trail, which is packed with snow that turns to slush in the sun and ice in the shade.

Although it's all downhill from Emmigrant Gap (shown above), the course does not become any easier.

In a race through the wilderness, runners have to keep their wits about them so they will not stray off course and get lost. In 1983, when the snow was especially deep, dozens of runners wandered off the trail and spent up to an hour trying to find it again.

At 32 miles—almost 6 miles further than a marathon—the racers reach their *first* checkpoint. By this time, several runners have usually dropped out because of massive blisters, broken ribs or sprains from falls, or the frustration of getting lost. From that point, the craggy trails wind down toward the canyons. With their feet still wet from the snow, the racers plunge into the 100-degree heat of the canyons.

On the racers go, past Duncan Canyon and Deep Canyon. Near the halfway point, they tackle the steepest part of the course, a two-mile stretch that carries them to a check point at Devil's Thumb. In 1985, an accurate measurement of the course revealed that it was short of 100 miles. That prompted race officials to introduce a new, even more rugged 16-mile section that year, beginning at mile 62. If runners are still inclined to continue, they plod through dusty, hot

No Hands Bridge is a welcome sight to all runners. It means that they have only 3.4 miles left before their ordeal is over.

flats that seem to be in the middle of nowhere. Finally, they may reach a sign of civilization, No Hands Bridge, which seems far too narrow and high for dazed runners to be crossing so late in the run. For slower runners, this last part of the race is by far the most dangerous. Numb from exhaustion, they have to pick their way in the dark over a narrow, rocky trail.

Those fortunate enough to have survived enter the town of Auburn. After the spectacular journey they have endured, they finish with what is probably the dullest and most routine quarter-mile in the world—a lap around a high school track. Roughly one-third of the contestants never reach this point. But for those who do, it can be an extremely emotional moment, and many have run their final lap in tears. Although prize money is now available to the winners,

Walking is not only for sissies in this race. Most runners know better than to waste their legs on the uphill portion of the course.

most Western States 100 racers are more than satisfied to carry home the silver belt buckle given to all finishers, along with the thrill of knowing they made it through the world's toughest course.

Those who run to win, however, can find the thrills and agonies of competition almost too much to take. Even the best runners have pushed their bodies to the limit of human ability only to see all their effort go to waste. In 1979, Doug Latimer held the lead for over 11 hours until, finally, his body couldn't take it anymore. Only 6 miles from the finish, he saw his victory dreams dashed as he was passed. Anyone who takes on the Western States 100, however, is not easily discouraged. Latimer was back in 1981 and tied for first place with his friend Jim Howard in a course record of 16 hours, 2 minutes, and 37 seconds.

In 1983, 26-year-old Jim King turned in the most impressive performance ever, yet came in second. Defying the experts by refusing to slow down to a walk even on the steepest climbs, King led the race early in the run by more than one-half hour. Unfortunately, he missed

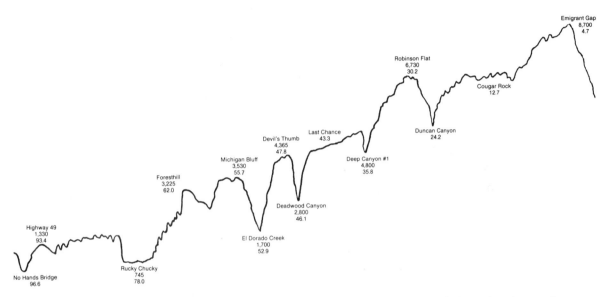

Emigrant Gap
8,700
4.7

Robinson Flat
6,730
30.2

Cougar Rock
12.7

Last Chance
43.3

Duncan Canyon
24.2

Devil's Thumb
4,365
47.8

Michigan Bluff
3,530
55.7

Deep Canyon #1
4,800
35.8

Foresthill
3,225
62.0

Deadwood Canyon
2,800
46.1

Highway 49
1,330
93.4

El Dorado Creek
1,700
52.9

Rucky Chucky
745
78.0

No Hands Bridge
96.6

The race course (running from right to left) starts with a backbreaking climb to Emmigrant Gap and continues with 100 miles of the world's toughest running terrain.

a turn and found himself completely lost in the wilderness. Although it took nearly an hour before he finally worked his way back to the course, King still made up enough ground to come within 31 seconds of the first-place finisher, who was again Jim Howard. Had he been able to stick to the course, King would have shattered the 1981 record set by Howard and Latimer. King more than made up for that loss in 1984, however. While one of his main competitors,

Barney Klecker, was done in by a wrong turn, King blazed the course in a record time of 14 hours, 54 minutes, and 19 seconds. By the time the second-place runner set foot on the track, King had been resting for nearly an hour. The next year, however, King straggled in more than one and one-half hours behind the new champ, Chuck Jones.

The scene at the finish of a Western States 100 ought to be enough to discourage anyone thinking of attempting

the race in the future. Racers are sprawled on cots or in sleeping bags on the infield of the track, unable to move. Even after drinking an incredible 45 quarts of liquid during the race, they still suffer nausea from dehydration. Some are having blisters treated while others are being handfed by friends or family. But despite their discomfort— even agony—these runners would swear that in all the world, there is no other organized footrace quite like the Western States 100.

A runner's only reward for surviving this harrowing test is a long, glorious sleep (above) and a silver belt buckle (below).

Defying the course and the 100-degree (Fahrenheit) temperatures right to the end, 1984 winner Jim King still had enough spring in his legs to leap across the finish line.

Some of the lucky 1,000 chosen to run the Pike's Peak Marathon begin to feel the effects of thin high-altitude air.

★★★ 3 ★★★
The Pike's Peak Marathon

In 1806, an explorer named Zebulon Pike made an all-out effort to climb a mountain peak in Colorado. Finally, he had to admit he couldn't find a way to get to the top. The frustrated Pike declared that "Pike's Peak" was so steep and treacherous that no man would ever be able to climb it.

Zebulon Pike would choke on his words if he could visit his famous mountain one weekend in August. Then, he would discover that people can not only reach the top, but as many as 1,000 clog the trail at one time, trying to get there first! He would, no doubt, be shocked to see runners cover the 14 miles from Manitou Springs to Pike's Peak in just over two hours. And he would probably be speechless when he saw them turn around and, without stopping, race the 14 miles back down the mountain!

Although it is "only" a marathon, and not an ultramarathon, the Pike's Peak Marathon race is hardly a picnic. It is the showcase event in the exhausting sport of mountain running, a North American sport for nearly 100 years. The Colorado mountains have been used as race courses since the Kendell Run back in the 1890s. This run up and down a mountain near Silverton, Colorado, was the wild idea of some restless miners who were looking for ways to put a little excitement into their free time. Miners considered the race more of a dare than an athletic event, and a good number of them had to drink themselves into a stupor before they would venture out onto the strenuous course.

Informal races up Pike's Peak started back in 1936, long before the current craze of long-distance challenges began. Twenty years later, a medical doctor

Explorer Zebulon Pike. Every year his "unclimbable" peak is overrun by waves of fitness buffs.

Universe—won that 1956 race. There has been a Pike's Peak Marathon held every year since, making it the second oldest annual marathon in the United States.

The thought of racing up the spectacular mountain that inspired Katherine Lee Bates to write "America, the Beautiful" appealed to more and more racers every year. By 1975, 350 contestants had joined the race, and organizers began to worry about crowding. After all, the out-and-back race course followed a narrow, steep trail that could cause a dangerous bottleneck after the halfway point, when some runners would be going down while slower ones were still ascending. The event was finally divided into two races. Eight hundred runners were allowed to enter the full, 28-mile marathon, and others would run a separate, 14-mile race to the top of the peak.

Each year, the race starts at 7:00 A.M. at Manitou Springs, a resort town overlooking Colorado Springs. Even this lowest point in the race is perched 6,336 feet above sea level. Contestants are advised to arrive at least a week ahead to get their bodies used to the thin air at that altitude.

The marathoners trot down paved

from Florida was looking for a way to prove smoking harmful to health, so he invited smokers and nonsmokers to take part in an experimental race to the top of Pike's Peak. No matter how bizarre the athletic challenge, there always seems to be at least 14 hardy souls who show up to give it a try, and the Pike's Peak race was no exception. Not surprisingly, the doctor's theory on smoking was proven correct, and a non-smoker—who later won the title of Mr.

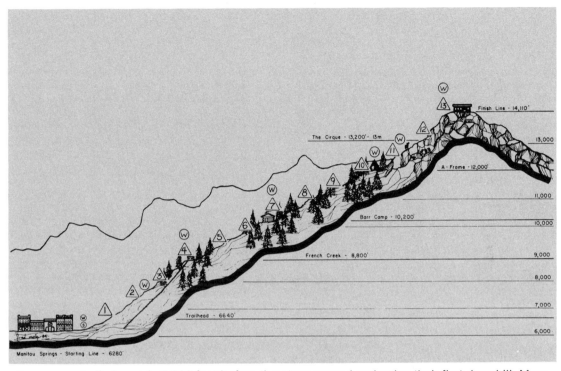

The Cirque - 13,200' - 13m

Finish Line - 14,110'

13,000

A - Frame - 12,000'

11,000

Barr Camp - 10,200'

10,000

French Creek - 8,800'

9,000

8,000

Trailhead - 6640'

7,000

6,000

Manitou Springs - Starting Line - 6280'

Racers must climb nearly 8,000 feet before they turn around and enjoy their first downhill. Many runners believe the strain of running downhill is even harder on leg muscles than the uphill.

roads for one and one-half miles before reaching Barr Trail. This is the old burro path, rough and narrow and full of boulders and loose rocks, that leads to Pike's Peak. Long before they even see Pike's Peak, however, the runners have to scale Mt. Manitou. Four miles of rugged switchbacks through scrub oak and aspen forest and then a jaunt through an evergreen forest lead them to Barr Camp, the halfway point. From there, the runners get their first look at Pike's Peak, which seems to rise to an impossible, intimidating height.

Summoning up all their courage, racers continue their climb to the upper parts of the course, where the lack of water can present severe problems. During most years, runners can drink from a number of cold, spring-fed streams. But there have been dry years when race officials have had to use burros to lug hundreds of gallons of water to refreshment points.

Gloves and shorts seem a strange combination, but Pike's Peak runners have to be prepared for both heat and cold.

After leaving Barr Camp, runners climb through Dismal Forest, filled with its eerie, scorched tree trunks, before finally passing the last of the trees. At that altitude—about 12,000 feet—the air is so thin that the shortest jog can leave a person gasping for breath. The worst part for racers is a steep stretch known as the 16 Golden Stairs. If the runners can keep from getting too dizzy or groggy, they will see a breathtaking view. Often, they can look down on patches of white clouds among the mountains as they wind toward the top.

Finally, the gasping racers reach the 14,110-foot peak, nearly one and one-half miles higher than their starting point. At that altitude, their quivering muscles are not helped by the temperatures that rarely rise much above freezing, even in the middle of summer. Bodies have trouble adjusting to the summer heat of Manitou Springs, then to the frosty conditions at the top, and, finally, back to 80 degrees (Fahrenheit) at the bottom.

Serious runners take no time to enjoy the world-famous view from the top of Pike's Peak, however, for they must immediately turn around and start the trip back down. That journey uses a

Race spectators enjoy a breathtaking view from the mountaintop. Runners at this point, however, have no breath to spare.

different set of muscles than the uphill run. Although it might seem to be a snap to let gravity carry the runner downhill, serious problems can arise on the return trip. Trying to keep under control while going down a steep hill can be very hard on the legs. The trail is rocky and uneven, and the danger of a bad fall is far greater for someone running downhill. This is especially true when legs become so heavy from fatigue they are hard to control.

In very tiring races through wilderness areas, there is also the danger of getting lost. After each Pike's Peak Marathon, search-and-rescue teams must scout the entire mountainside to find anyone who has wandered off course.

The first Pike's Peak Marathon was won in 5 hours and 39 minutes. Today's best runners can reach the top in a little over 2 hours and can finish the entire 28-mile race in less than 3½ hours. The race has produced its own heroes,

35

such as five-time race champion Rick Trujillo and record-smashing Al Waquie. One of the most heroic Pike's Peak Marathon runners was a woman who completed the course 13 times and then died during her 14th race, at the age of 88. And if the Pike's Peak Marathon is a stiff challenge for a person in perfect health, consider the determination of one runner who has completed the race several times despite the handicap of being born without feet. People such as those Pike's Peak racers have shown how much Zebulon Pike underestimated the determination of his fellow humans.

Colorful Al Waquie, a frequent winner at Pike's Peak, had cemented his reputation as one of the world's fastest climbers by winning a 1983 race up the stairs of New York's 102-story Empire State Building in 11 minutes and 36 seconds.

Once a year, the beauty of the Colorado mountains is littered with the debris of humans determined to challenge the might of nature.

In a country teeming with racial tension, the **Comrades Marathon** offers a welcome release for thousands of runners of all backgrounds, ages, and sizes.

4

The Comrades Marathon

While it may not wreak quite the destruction on humans as the Western States 100, South Africa's Comrades Marathon is the oldest and most successful organized ultramarathon road race in the world. Because of the great number of participants, this race can probably claim to have caused more voluntary human suffering than any other athletic event in the world.

Compared to the other races in this book, the Comrades is more a test of people vs. nature than a race against the clock or a rival. Most of the competitors encourage each other to keep up their spirits during the race. Throughout the hill-riddled, 90-kilometer (about 54 miles) course, spectators come out to cheer and to support the brave souls who are struggling to fulfill their dream of completing the famous Comrades course. The marathon even brings about

a temporary easing of South Africa's rigid separation of blacks and whites, as everyone is allowed to run together in one single, massive event.

The Comrades was started back in 1921 for reasons a little more noble than most of the other races in this book. It was not a dare, a lark, a whim, or an ego trip. Instead, it was an event set up by some South African veterans of World War I to honor their comrades who had died in the war. The race has always followed the same course, a road connecting the coastal city of Durban with the town of Pietermaritzburg in the interior highlands. The one twist is that the course changes direction every year. One year, the race is run from Pietermaritzburg down to Durban, and, the next year, it is run from Durban to Pietermaritzburg. Less stout-hearted souls wait for the "down" years when

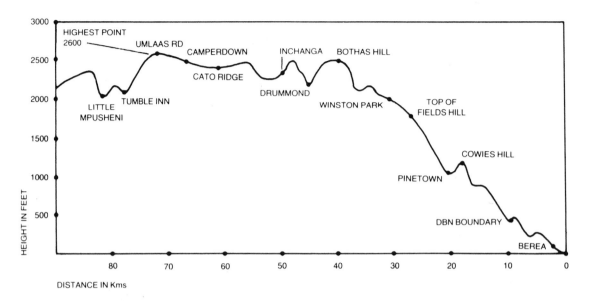

Above: the Comrades Marathon race course extends from Durban (point 0 on map) to Pieter-maritzburg. Depending on the year, the race either begins or ends in the modern seacoast city of Durban (below).

the course is supposed to be easier. But when the 2,000-foot drop in elevation from Pietermaritzburg to Durban is spread over 54 miles of endless hills, most runners wouldn't know which way was up or down!

Like many of the world's strangest runs, this one started out as a quiet, friendly affair. Only men participated, and often their wives and families or girlfriends would take the whole day off to help them and follow them in a vehicle. This tradition was so strong that it wasn't until 1981 when "seconds" —people riding or driving alongside a runner—were banned from the race. The first marathon in 1921 was won in a leisurely time of 8 hours and 59 minutes The second race was won by a 39-year-old farmer who had only recently taken up running as a way of protest. Arthur Newton ran the Comrades to publicize his complaint against the government for taking his land, and he followed his 1922 upset win with victories in 1923, 1924, 1925, and 1927.

The competition in memory of fallen soldiers was called off during the years of World War II. During that war, an ex-Comrades champion, Bill Cochrane, was taken prisoner by the Germans. After escaping, he struggled through a brutal trip to freedom, which took him on foot through Poland and the Soviet Union. While most men might have dreamed of a hot bath or a five-course dinner during that terrible time, Cochrane kept himself going by vowing if and when he ever returned home, he would run the Comrades Marathon. Cochrane not only made good on his promise but also took first place in the first post-war Comrades in 1946. Typical of the more relaxed training programs at that time, Bill ran only three times a week, even during his peak training season.

Since then, however, the Comrades has mushroomed in size, and the competition has grown fierce. Never was it more gripping than in the "down" race of 1967. After nearly 54 miles of full effort, Manny Kuhn still had enough energy left to sprint the last 150 meters (about 500 feet). That frantic finishing kick gave him a fraction-of-a-second victory over his main competitor.

Currently, the Comrades Marathon attracts a field of more than 7,000 runners, including many world-class athletes

Despite the presence of refreshment stands every 1.5 kilometers (.09 mile), the greatest danger to runners is dehydration under the relentless sun.

from many countries. With so many racers spread out over 90 kilometers of road, keeping order and maintaining safety becomes a massive job. For the 1981 race, more than 1,600 volunteers manned their posts at 58 refreshment stands and 68 sponging points. Hot, sweaty racers went through 160,000 bottles of drinking water, 45,000 liters (11,700 gallons) of Coca-Cola, and 60,000 sponges. In addition, each station was stocked with 3,000 liters (780 gallons) of water and several tons of ice.

Even with all these liquids available, heat-related injuries are common during the race. Although the Comades is generally run in May—which is late autumn in the southern hemisphere—the midday sun can be very hot. Over the years, several runners have suffered kidney failure because of the extreme lack of liquids. All competitors are urged to keep drinking throughout the race, even if they do not feel thirsty.

Although the Comrades Marathon had been around for more than 60 years, its novelty has not begun to wear off. Along the race course, spectators still do their best to encourage those who have decided to give this famous race

Bruce Fordyce had the applause all to himself as he won his fourth straight Comrades' title in 1984.

a try. Somehow, its hospitality and largeness help people to fulfill their dream of finishing. Although the race is wide open to even the least experienced runners, over 95 percent of the starters manage to stay on their feet to the end. Judging by the huge number of people who run in the race year after year, probably no other race in the world has brought about so much satisfaction and as many long-distance running addicts as the Comrades.

**Leaving Arctic Bay behind, Nanisivik Midnight Sun contestants push on through the eerie
silence of an Arctic wasteland.**

★★★ 5 ★★★
The Nanisivik Midnight Sun Ultra

The Inuit word *nanisivik* means "place where people find things." For people who are hunting for experiences of unbelievable fatigue, pain, and satisfaction, the town of Nanisivik is certainly the place to find it. Since 1978, this tiny mining community, tucked 480 miles north of the Arctic Circle, has hosted the annual Nanisivik Midnight Sun Ultra. Along with the shorter races, which includes a marathon, the program features an 84-kilometer (about a 50.5-mile) ultramarathon that has shaken some of the toughest runners in the world.

Unlike the Comrades Marathon, the Midnight Sun Ultra attracts only diehard ultramarathon buffs. There simply aren't many people who would shell out $500 for a flight from Montreal, Canada, to the middle of nowhere for *any* reason, much less to run their bodies into the ground. Ultramarathoning, however, does not necessarily have much to do with sanity. Even for this remote race on the northwest tip of the virtually desolate Baffin Island, runners have to get in line early if they want to be included in the race. Because there is very little housing available, the Midnight Sun challenges are limited to the first 85 entrants.

Were it not for the murderous 50 miles that Ultra contestants are expected to run, it might be a fun vacation. People who love travel would find it thrilling to step out on a land that is far north of Iceland and is closer to the North Pole than to the northernmost tip of Alaska. All entrants are graciously housed with some of the town's hearty zinc miners or in the few government houses set up in the area. There they can explore an eerie, vast wasteland seen by few travelers.

The Midnight Sun races were dreamed

Veteran ultramarathoner Arctic Joe Womersley—
also shown on page 42—kicked off the first
Midnight Sun Ultra in 1980 with a second place
finish.

up by a retired Canadian businessman, Joe Womersley, who had spent enough time in the frigid zones to be known as Arctic Joe. An avid runner himself, he has worked hard to make runners comfortable when not running—and extremely uncomfortable while running! The race's claim to be the world's toughest marathon is based on something most runners take for granted: the running surface. Nanisivik is connected to the small Inuit village of Arctic Bay by a road made of crushed rock. Ultra runners know they won't be able to count on one step of smooth, solid surface throughout the entire race. The discouraging surface, the long distance, and the steep hills have convinced many distance runners to avoid the ultra and try one of the shorter races instead. In 1983, only 11 brave souls stepped forward to attempt the long run—and 4 of them had to be talked into it at the last minute!

The Midnight Sun Ultra follows the road from Nanisivik to Arctic Bay and back. A uniformed Royal Canadian Mounted Police handles the starting chores and sends the racers on their way toward the Arctic Ocean. Here

Racers receive last-minute instructions before starting their journey. At least they don't have to worry about getting lost as the course has only one turn.

runners don't have to worry about the temperature. Even though the race is held at the peak of summer, weather conditions during the world's northernmost race fall in the comfortable running range of 25 to 65 degrees (Fahrenheit).

Long-distance running is at least as much a mental strain as it is physical,

and that can cause extra problems during the Midnight Sun Ultra. Racers have no way of knowing what to expect from a run through an arctic desert until they experience the sensation of running through a world that appears to be nothing but a pile of rock. Trees are unheard of in that climate; the hills are

Nanisivik
Midnight Sun Marathon
BAFFIN ISLAND
CANADA

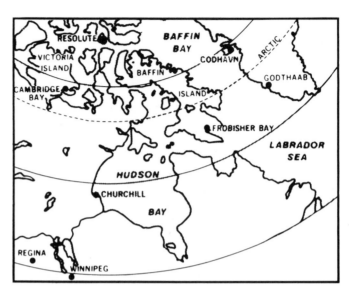

COURSE PROFILE

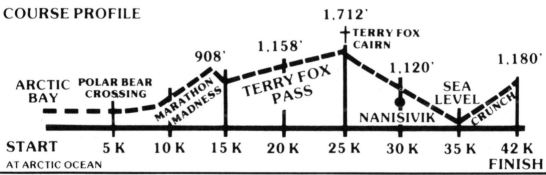

Although run at close to sea level, this course on the northern-most tip of Baffin Island is far from flat.

totally barren except for a few tiny flowers that bloom only briefly. This bleak landscape makes it almost impossible to gauge distances between landmarks. Nothing is more discouraging to runners than working hard to reach a hill that seems to be three miles away

only to find, after three miles, that the hill looks to be no closer than it was at the start!

Also, distance runners are used to being encouraged–or sometimes heckled–by spectators. In Nanisivik, a small band of racers run in a place so remote they could travel hundreds of miles in any direction and never see a sign of civilization. For almost the entire run, racers will hear no sounds of life other than their own breathing and footsteps and the continuous, haunting howl of the wind blowing unchecked over the land. When there is so little to occupy the mind, a long run can seem to take forever.

Although the amount of hill climbing in the Midnight Sun Ultra does not approach the outlandish requirements of some other runs in this book, an Ultra runner must still expect to face a total climb of about 6,500 feet. Race organizers have saved the toughest section for the end. The trail rises 1,000 feet during the final three miles, a stretch known as The Crunch. As an example of how tough the gravel course is on racers, compare the Midnight Sun Marathon record to that of any other marathon. While world-class marathoners usually finish a course in under 2 hours and 10 minutes, the best time for the Midnight Sun is just under 3 hours. Some of the United State's best ultramarathoners have said the course is tougher than Pike's Peak.

It's a long way to come for a workout, but this Ultra contestant believes it is worth the effort.

The spirit of the Midnight Sun run is best shown by the decision to name the highest stretch of the course Terry Fox Pass. Terry Fox was a 21-year-old Canadian cancer victim who was determined to run across Canada. Although he had lost a leg to the disease, he ran 26 miles (the equivalent of a marathon) every day for five months before losing his battle for life. Despite the incredibly tough course conditions, every starter in the 1983 race made it to the finish line. The entrants did an incredible job of living up to the race motto that was inspired by Fox: "He never gave up."

Courageous Terry Fox raised millions of dollars for cancer research by running halfway across Canada on one leg. His unbeatable spirit is memorialized by Terry Fox Pass.

★★★ 6 ★★★

The Torturous 26

When asked why there were 508 men but only 32 women registered for the 1983 St. Paul (Minnesota) Torturous 26, one race official responded, "Apparently women have more sense." While this marathon is run over a much easier course than the other races in this book, it introduces a factor that runners seem to dread more than anything else: Winter!

Even runners who are used to the cold fret about how to keep in shape during a northern winter, and serious runners often move to warmer climates so they don't have to put up with the snow and the cold. Although thousands of cooler-climate runners flock to races in the brutal heat of Hawaii or the Western canyons, few southerners feel the urge to run through a northern blizzard. Part of this is fear of the unknown. Most people have been unbearably hot some-time in their lives, but few know what it's like to spend several hours in minus-40-degree (Fahrenheit) weather. The other fear is of *really* bad race conditions. What if a storm hits so hard on race day that the snowplows have to be pulled off the streets?

The dangers that winter presents to the unfamiliar is best illustrated by a California triathlete named Sally Edwards. Although Edwards had the courage to venture into the northland for the 1983 race and outdid the locals to win the women's division, she nearly committed a horrible mistake during the race. As she cruised by a refreshment stand, she took a sip of water and then automatically started to do what athletes have been doing in marathons for years: she started to splash the rest of the water in the cup on her face. Fortunately, she caught herself in time to avoid the shock of her life—and the danger of frostbite!

Frosted right down to his eyelashes, this runner nevertheless enjoyed the challenge of The Freeze Yer Gizzard Blizzard Run.

The Torturous 26 race is relatively new. It was first held in 1982 when the annual St. Paul Winter Carnival was looking for an event to replace a cross-country snowmobile race, and someone suggested they take advantage of the popularity of foot races. Although St. Paul could be frigid in early February, carnival officials knew they wouldn't be able to claim that their race was held in the world's coldest location. The northern Minnesota community of International Falls—where in January the thermometer breaks 0 degrees (Fahrenheit) only during warm spells—already held a popular 10-kilometer race (about 6 miles), the Freeze Yer Gizzard Blizzard Run. But St. Paul would host the first cold-climate marathon in midwinter.

Runners who looked forward to this race as a novel test of human will must have been pleased by the first race in 1982. That year, temperatures plunged to more than 10 degrees below zero, with a wind chill index of minus 30 degrees. Such weather, however, sounds worse than it really is, for, with careful preparation, runners would run very little risk of weather-related injury.

Although they are carrying far more baggage than most marathon runners, these runners don't have to worry about overheating.

The starting line that year looked like a clothing store advertisement for long underwear, sweaters, mittens, and hats. Along with several layers of light clothing and petroleum jelly smeared over exposed areas of their faces, the runners were all set. National Ski Patrol members were scattered on the course, and churches and mortuaries were recruited for safety stations. A bus tagged along with the last of the runners to make sure no one suffered too badly from the cold. Doctors assured participants that unless temperatures dipped to around minus 80 degrees, they didn't have to worry about the cold air damaging their lungs. Actually, because dehydration, the main enemy of ultra-runners, would not be a factor, the race was less risky than most. Of the 216 starters, 169 finished, and none complained about conditions being too bad for running.

One of the worst features of winter running is trying to find traction on road that's completely covered with snow.

Winter running does pose a few unusual problems for both racers and officials, however, as no one has yet invented a running shoe that can glide easily over a combination of snow, glare ice, slush, and dry pavement. Slippery surfaces are not only fatiguing, they can cause falls that result in injuries. Winter race officials, meanwhile, had to experiment with ways to keep liquids at refreshment stands from freezing and to get finishing times and places logged without freezing their fingers.

When St. Paul police requested the route be changed after the first race, the Torturous 26 start and finish point was moved to the St. Paul Downtown Airport. Race officials added to the challenge of the run by including one long climb at the start of the race and another one about halfway through, when the course winds through such varied terrain as scenic Como Park and busy downtown St. Paul.

The dislike that many distance runners hold for winter shows up in the 26's winner's circle. In 1982, 1983, and 1984, the men's division winner was not a world-reknowned athlete, but a local runner. In 1983, in fact, the event was

Ever searching for unusual challenges, this group tackled the Torturous 26 while hooked together in a centipede costume.

won by a man who had never finished a marathon before. That is not to say, however, the idea of a winter marathon is too ridiculous to attract a following. In the event's second year, the number of contestants more than doubled and included a group of 13 men running together in a costume of a 60-foot green centipede! In 1984, more than 1,000 runners showed up to battle the cold.

While runners were willing to brave the worst that winter could offer, race officials were not. In 1986, the race was chopped to a half-marathon. Such world-class runners as Dick Beardsley, winner of the 1987 contest, no longer had a Torturous 26 to look forward to. Odd as it may seem, there was an army of runners who believed that cutting the distance in half made winter only half as much fun!

Park rangers would prefer that Bright Angel Trail be left to hikers and mules, but they can't stop adventurous runners from tackling another bizarre challenge.

7

The Grand Canyon Double Traverse

The United States National Park Service gives millions of people a chance to view some of the most breathtaking scenery in the world. These parks are meant to be enjoyed and studied at a leisurely pace, and park officials have always been concerned with the safety of park visitors.

It seems, however, that some people cannot stand a leisurely pace. They want the parks to be "breathtaking" all right, and they do that by turning fascinating nature trails into a race course. Safety-conscious park rangers have refused to allow an organized trail run through the Grand Canyon, but that hasn't stopped hundreds of runners from taking a crack at one of the world's most dangerous endurance tests, the Grand Canyon Double Traverse.

The Double Traverse is simply a run from the north rim to the bottom of the canyon, then up the south rim and doubling back to the beginning. Since there are no organized races and no way that the narrow treacherous, trails could accomodate a pack of runners, this is a race against the clock, not other people. It is also a race against the trail itself and the climate.

The very hazards that make group racing impossible make it extremely dangerous for small groups or individual runners. Rain storms can wash out sections of the trail, and fallen and falling rocks pose a risk, even in dry weather. Footing on the packed dirt trail is often insecure, and one false step can send a runner plummeting to his or her death over the sheer, dizzying drop-offs that line the trail as it winds down into the mile-deep canyon. Many people would feel queasy just walking the trail, let alone running along it.

Spectacular scenery rewards the runner while he or she is still fresh enough to enjoy it.

The Grand Canyon's hostile climate is made even more dangerous by the absence of supervision. Other races are monitored by officials so runners in trouble can get help quickly, or they have refreshment stands along the race course so runners have a chance to combat dehydration. But there is no such assistance in the Grand Canyon. Runners go into the canyon knowing no volunteers are waiting for them. Over the years, many hikers have not returned when they were supposed to, and desperate search parties—some successful and some not—have spent days hunting for them. Imagine then the risks a runner takes when racing all-out in this desert environment.

The idea of a timed rim-to-rim run first became popular in 1976. That same year, Max Telford, an ultramarathoner from New Zealand, topped that feat with a round trip run, the first double traverse. Telford completed his run after what may have seemed like the longest 8 hours and 34 minutes he had ever spent. Now it's estimated that more than 200 runners travel to the Grand Canyon each year to follow in his footsteps. Competitive runners aim for the lofty goal of

Narrow, hazardous trails such as the North Kaibab Trail, 17 miles into the run, have restricted the Grand Canyon Double Reverse to an individual race against the clock.

finishing in under 8 hours; others are satisfied just to complete the run. During the last organized race in 1981, 49 runners completed the course in under 15 hours.

Knowing the beastly hot conditions that lie at the bottom of the canyon, one would expect runners to venture out only during the cool months of the year. Unfortunately, nature sees to it that no one avoids the heat. The trail starts at an altitude of over 8,000 feet on the north rim, which is snowbound —and, therefore, inexcessible—from as early as October until as late as May.

During the summer months when the trail is open, runners are likely to start under very mild, pleasant conditions and can enjoy the splendor of the world's largest canyon. Red, polished cliffs

In such a forbidding environment, water breaks are more than welcome. They are a matter of life and death.

surround them as they wind downward, and there is never a shortage of beautiful and unusual lime and sandstone formations. At the very bottom, they can get a close look at some black rock that is the oldest exposed rock on the earth.

Most runners find, however, that they can risk no more than a peek every now and then as they go up and down the rims. The trail is often a narrow ledge, no wider than 4 to 8 feet. At times, it plunges down at a 35 percent grade (dropping 35 feet for every 100 feet forward), and runners have to fight to keep gravity from pushing them out of control. Racers also have to watch so they don't suddenly bump into the many hikers or mule trains traveling in the opposite direction. In the Grand Canyon, mule trains have the right of way, and runners must stand quietly aside while they pass.

At the bottom of the canyon, the trail crosses and recrosses a narrow stream, and then it leads over a suspension bridge across the Colorado River. The agreeable starting conditions will have long since passed, and runners find themselves in a true desert.

This footbridge spanning the Colorado River offers another reason why those afraid of heights are advised not to attempt the Double Traverse.

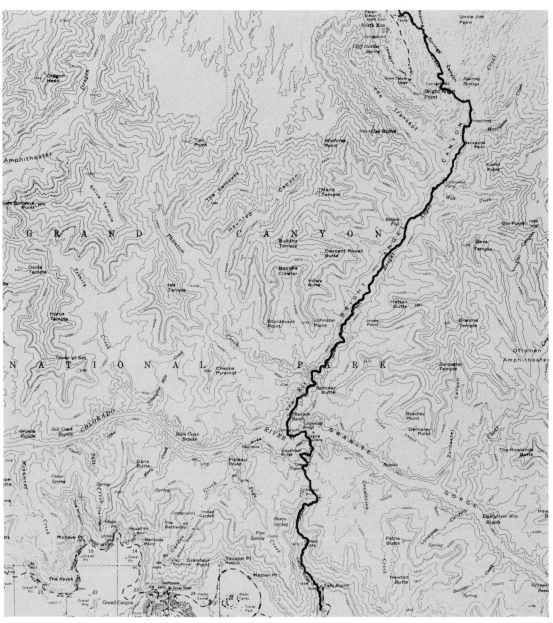

When traced on a map, the Double Traverse route—starting and ending at the North Rim—gives no indication of either the beauty or the harsh environment that surrounds the runner.

There is no hope that even a moment of shade will break the grip of temperatures that climb to over 100 degrees (Fahrenheit), even in moderate seasons, and reach 120 degrees in the summer. Running in that kind of heat is more than uncomfortable; it is also very dangerous. In extreme temperatures, blood cannot circulate effectively, and damage to major organs is possible.

Runners must either carry plenty of water with them or stash it along the trail ahead of time. On the hottest and driest stretch, the South Kaibab Trail, no water can to be found for over six miles. Rangers have had to deal with as many as 150 heat-related emergencies every year, and many of the victims had to be carried out by mule or by helicopter.

Runners finally face a steep climb up the south rim—the last seven miles leave them a mile higher than they were at the bottom. By the time they reach Yaki Point, they will have traveled 20.6 miles. Then they have to turn around and cover the same ground all over again. By this time, many runners are likely to agree with the National Park Service: the Grand Canyon is meant to be enjoyed at a leisurely pace!

The majestic splendor of the Grand Canyon masks the danger that awaits any person who enters unprepared.

Even the most experienced ultramarathoners seem like beginners when compared with these iron-legged racers from the Tarahumara Mountains of Mexico.

★★★ 8 ★★★
The Rarahipa

No book about ultramarathons could be complete without mentioning the private races that take place high in the Tarahumara Mountains of Mexico. While ultramarathons may seem like utter madness to some people, to the Tarahumara Indians, they are a part of everyday life. It is as common to see them taking part in a 100-mile run as to see baseball being played in the United States. The race that they call *rarahipa* is actually a game to them.

No one knows how many centuries have passed since the first rarahipa was staged high in these rugged Mexican mountains, 400 miles south of El Paso, Texas. There are no records of winners and no official time or exact distance raced. The event consists of teams kicking a wooden ball as they run and run and run, and it could be considered the ultimate running contest because

so few people, no matter how well-conditioned they are, ever finish a rarahipa. Only one person can finish a race because, according to the rules, the race goes on until only one person is able to continue. The superhuman endurance of the Tarahumara racers guarantees that it will be days before that finally happens.

Running is so important to this group of Mexicans that they call themselves the Raramuri, which means "footrunners." They are related to the Apache Indians living in the southwestern United States. The Apaches often astounded their enemies by appearing 75 miles from where they had been the day before without using horses.

There are fewer than 50,000 Raramuri –or Tarahumaras, as they are more commonly called–and they are not easy to find. After war and mistreatment at

Tucked away in their mountain homes, the Tarahumaras manage to avoid interference from most outsiders.

the hands of settlers in the 17th century, they retreated deep into the rugged, roadless canyons of the mountains. Withdrawn and suspicious of outsiders, their lives have changed little over the past 300 years. They live in huts and caves as their ancestors did, and they still run everywhere.

In 1890, a Norwegian naturalist ventured into Raramuri territory and came back with what seemed like ridiculous stories. Who would believe there were people who could stand all day long without moving a muscle as they waited for some game animal to come within range of their crude weapons? How likely was it that these Tarahumaras really sent messengers on 50-mile jaunts through the steep, rocky land and chased after deer in relay teams

This group of Tarahumara runners was photographed in 1915.

until the animal dropped from exhaustion? Had the naturalist really seen a group of Raramuri easily cover 40 miles within six hours?

Later stories of Tarahumara endurance were even more incredible. One report told of a group of porters who hauled a piano 185 miles in 15 days and then turned around and dashed home in 3 days! Many shrugged these off as tall tales until several Tarahumara came to the United States in the 1920s to give demonstrations of their running. Sure enough, they completed a 65-mile journey in just over nine and one-half hours without showing signs of discomfort.

Naturally, sports fans expected these runners to dominate the Olympic marathons. When asked if they would be interested in competing in an official marathon, one village agreed and sent three runners—all young girls. Although they ran remarkably well, they did not win the race. When the Tarahumara were asked why they hadn't sent their best runners, they replied that when they heard the race was only 26 miles, they assumed it was for children! Because of the marathon's "shortness" and

A rarahipa ball may travel more than 200 miles over rocky ground before the contest is over.

because they are not interested in speed, the Tarahumara have never made a mark in world marathon competition.

The Tarahumara, however, have proven to be the greatest group of long-distance runners in the world. Their races are part of the village festivals held by the Tarahumara to celebrate all special occasions. Usually, one village will challenge another to a game or a race, the longest being the rarahipa. Runners from each team carve a ball about the size of a grapefruit from an oak branch. Then they lay out a course by cutting crosses in the bark of trees. There is no standard distance to a race loop, and the courses will vary from 3 to 12 miles in length. Because there is no chance the race will be over in one day, much of the race must be run in darkness, when pine torches are scattered to light the way. It is especially important that the contestants be able to see because if they lose their ball, they are disqualified. Race supervisors must watch to see that opponents do not boot someone else's ball out of sight.

Despite the exhausting demands of the race, the Tarahumara do not train for it. One reason is because they do

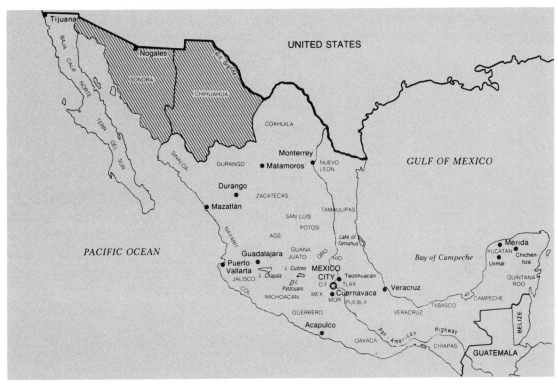

Tarahumara communities are located in the states of Chihuahua and Sonora in northern Mexico.

enough running in their daily routine to keep them in shape. But a more important reason is that they believe that magic, not conditioning, is what wins races. Losers are convinced their opponents have found ways to hex them. People from many of the villages are not above hiding bones along the course, because they believe that bones are capable of sapping a person's strength. Their runners, of course, are careful to avoid those spots.

On the day of the race, competitors are wrapped in blankets, and their legs are rubbed with warm water. At at signal from the starter, they throw off their wraps and start on their way. Although Tarahumara usually wear sandals when they run, they run the rarahipa barefoot so they can use their toes to flip the ball further. Supervisors follow along to keep the teams from bumping into each other or interfering with their progress. Spectators take an active part

A painting of a Tarahumara runner

in the event as well, shouting encouragement and helping to find a ball that rolls away.

For the first 40 miles or so, the race is easy and fun. Runners do not worry about the passage of time in the same way the Western world does and do not consider it boring to keep moving for such a long time. Gradually, runners begin to drop out until only the best runners remain. Even at this point, the race seems to take a greater toll on the ball than on the runners! By the time the race has finished, the rocky ground may have worn down the grapefruit-sized ball to the size of a golf ball.

Anyone preparing to watch a rarahipa contest would do well to bring along provisions—and had better not be in a hurry to get somewhere else! The contest may last for three days and the runners may travel more than 200 miles before the next-to-last man in the race finally gives up.

While a 200-mile race may not be most people's idea of a good time, the rarahipa races help to bring pleasure to a very poor group of people. Many Tarahumara children die in infancy, and, even in the best of times, there may be very little to eat. Considering their poor diet and the absence of any formal athletic training, the rarahipa winner may have already passed the most strenuous test of human endurance.

These Tarahumara children are likely to grow up in a world that will not be much different from that of their ancestors.

NATE AASENG, author of more than 70 books for young readers, took a special interest in researching this book. A long-distance runner in high school and in college, Aaseng has experienced that indescribable feeling of "hitting the wall" in a marathon race and has endured the taunts of those who thought he was crazy for enduring it. Although he runs shorter distances now—and purely for enjoyment—Aaseng is still young enough to gaze with envy at the knights who set off to conquer these punishing ultramarathons, and yet old enough to wonder about the strange inner urgings that make someone want to do such a thing!

ACKNOWLEDGMENTS: The photographs and maps are reproduced through the courtesy of: pp. 1, 10, 13, 14, 15, 16, 17, Hawaiian Triathlon Corporation; pp. 2, 6, 30, 34, 35, 36, 37, Nancy Hobbs; pp. 8, 50, UPI/Bettmann Newsphotos; pp. 18, 24, 27, 28 (right), Western States 100; p. 20, Marlene Degrood, PHOTOWORKS, Dutch Flat, CA; pp. 21, 23, 28 (top), PHOTOWORKS; pp. 22, 29, Hughes Photography; p. 26, Barieau; p. 32, *Dictionary of American Portraits*; p. 33, Triple Crown of Running; pp. 38, 43, Embassy of South Africa; p. 40 (top), Comrades Marathon; p. 40 (bottom), SATOUR; pp. 42, 44, 46, 47, 49, Joe Womersley; p. 49, Nanisivik Midnight Sun Marathon; p. 52, *The Daily Journal*, International Falls, MN; pp. 53 (Steve Deutsch Photography), 54, St. Paul Winter Carnival Association; p. 55, Edina Realty, Inc.; pp. 56, 61, 62, 63, Department of Interior, Grand Canyon National Park; pp. 58, 60, National Running Data Center, Inc.; p. 59, Fred Riemer; pp. 64, 68, Arizona State Museum, The University of Arizona, Thomas B. Hinton, Photographer; pp. 66, 70, Dick Bancroft; p. 67, Museum of New Mexico, Negative Number 46321; p. 69, Carol Barrett. Front cover: Marlene Degrood, PHOTOWORKS, Dutch Flat, CA. Back cover: Joe Womersley.